DETROIT PUBLIC LIBRARY

# *from* SEA TO SHINING SEA
# ARKANSAS

By Dennis Brindell Fradin and Judith Bloom Fradin

DETROIT PUBLIC LIBRARY

LINCOLN BRANCH LIBRARY
1221 E. SEVEN MILE
DETROIT, MI 48203

DATE DUE

John L. Fergus                                    ommission
Robert L. Hillerich                               ate University;

BC-3

APR -

D1225279

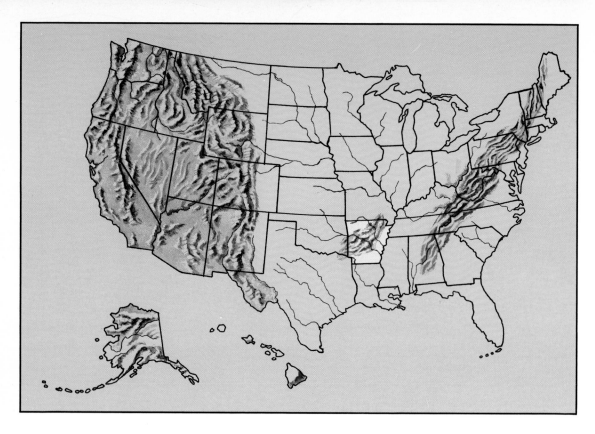

*Arkansas is one of the fourteen states in the region called the South. The other southern states are Alabama, Delaware, Florida, Georgia, Kentucky, Louisiana, Maryland, Mississippi, North Carolina, South Carolina, Tennessee, Virginia, and West Virginia.*

*For our dear aunt and uncle, Yetta and Sol Levita*

Front cover picture: The Old Mill, North Little Rock; page 1, Sunrise, Newton County; back cover: Cedar Creek Valley, Petit Jean State Park

Project Editor: Joan Downing
Design Director: Karen Kohn
Typesetting: Graphic Connections, Inc.
Engraving: Liberty Photoengraving

SECOND PRINTING, 1994.

Copyright © 1994 Childrens Press®, Inc.
All rights reserved. Published simultaneously in Canada.
Printed in the United States of America.
  2 3 4 5 6 7 8 9 10 R 03 02 01 00 99 98 97 96 95 94

Library of Congress Cataloging-in-Publication Data

Fradin, Dennis B.
  Arkansas / by Dennis Brindell Fradin and Judith Bloom
Fradin.
    p.   cm. — (From sea to shining sea)
  Includes index.
  ISBN 0-516-03804-4
  1. Arkansas—Juvenile literature. [1. Arkansas.] I. Title.
II. Series: Fradin, Dennis B. From sea to shining sea.
F411.3.F6   1994                              93-32677
976.7—dc20                                        CIP
                                                   AC

∠/   APR - - 1997

# Table of Contents

*Many children have their faces painted at Little Rock's Riverfest.*

# INTRODUCING THE LAND OF OPPORTUNITY

Arkansas's name is pronounced "AR-kun-saw." The name comes from *Akansea*. That means "south wind." *Akansea* was another name for the Quapaw Indians. Long ago, they lived in Arkansas.

Arkansas's nickname since 1953 has been "Land of Opportunity." The state has rich farming land. Arkansas leads the country at raising chickens and growing rice. Large deposits of oil and natural gas lie under the soil.

In recent years, many factories have been built in Arkansas. They make foods, machines, and paper goods. Tourism has also become an important industry. Each year, millions of visitors enjoy Arkansas's spring waters, mountains, and forests.

The Land of Opportunity is special in other ways. Where is the country's only diamond mine? What state's biggest city was named for a little rock? Where were baseball stars Lou Brock and Brooks Robinson born? What state elected the first woman to the United States Senate? Where was President Bill Clinton born? The answer to these questions is: Arkansas.

A picture map
of Arkansas

Overleaf: The
Cossatot River, in the
Ouachita Mountains

5

# Plains, Mountains, and Springs

# PLAINS, MOUNTAINS, AND SPRINGS

Arkansas is in the South. It is the farthest west of the southern states. Six states border Arkansas. Missouri is to the north. Tennessee and Mississippi are to the east. Louisiana lies to the south. Texas and Oklahoma are to the west.

The Land of Opportunity covers 53,187 square miles. About half of the fifty states are larger than Arkansas.

Eastern and southern Arkansas are made up of plains. These lands are rather low and level. Arkansas's best farmland is on the plains.

To the north and west are mountains and a deep valley. The Ozark Mountains are in northern Arkansas. Thick forests and livestock farms are found there. The Ouachita Mountains are in western and central Arkansas. Much coal and natural gas are under this land.

The Arkansas Valley lies between these two highlands. It has rich land. Magazine Mountain is in the Arkansas Valley. It is the state's highest point. Magazine Mountain stands 2,753 feet above sea level.

*Early spring in the Ouachita Mountains*

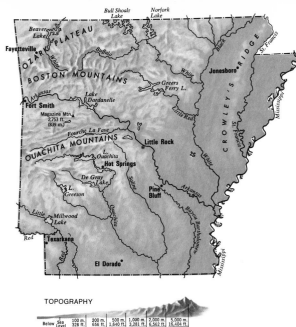

TOPOGRAPHY

| Below Sea Level | 100 m. 328 ft. | 200 m. 656 ft. | 500 m. 1,640 ft. | 1,000 m. 3,281 ft. | 2,000 m. 6,562 ft. | 5,000 m. 16,404 ft. |

## WATERS AND WOODLANDS

The Mississippi River forms Arkansas's border with Tennessee and Mississippi. Part of Arkansas's border with Missouri is made by the St. Francis River. The Red River forms part of the state's border with Texas.

The longest river inside Arkansas is the Arkansas. It flows eastward across the state from Fort Smith. The Arkansas empties into the Mississippi River north of Arkansas City. The Ouachita River snakes through southern Arkansas. The Strawberry, Black, and White are Arkansas rivers with colorful names.

Arkansas has many large artificially made lakes. They were formed by damming rivers. These lakes

*Left: Sunflowers and cypress trees near the mouth of the Arkansas River*

*The Arkansas River flows through Colorado, Kansas, and Oklahoma before it enters Arkansas.*

9

include Ouachita, Millwood, Greers Ferry, and Beaver. Lake Chicot is Arkansas's largest natural lake. It was formed when the Mississippi River changed its course.

Arkansas also has hundreds of springs. More than 200 million gallons of water bubble from them each day. Most of the springs are in Arkansas's mountains.

About half of Arkansas is wooded. Ozark, Ouachita, and Saint Francis national forests are in the state. The pine tree is the state tree. Hickory, maple, oak, willow, and wild cherry trees also grow in Arkansas.

## WILDLIFE

Black bears roam Arkansas's woods. Deer are common in the fields and woods. Twenty-pound bobcats prowl the highlands. Some armadillos live in Arkansas. Bony plates cover their bodies. A few alligators live in southern Arkansas swampland. Red foxes, opossums, raccoons, and woodchucks are also found in the state.

The mockingbird is the state bird. It mocks, or imitates, other birds' songs. The whippoorwill's song sounds like its name. Cardinals, robins, ducks,

*Arkansas has towns named Pine Bluff, Hickory Ridge, Oak Grove, Willow, and Wild Cherry.*

*Armadillo*

and wild turkeys are other birds in Arkansas. Trout, catfish, and buffalofish swim in Arkansas's lakes and rivers.

*Left: A view of Ozark National Forest from Hawksbill Crag
Right: Winter in the Ozarks*

## CLIMATE

Arkansas has a warm, wet climate. Temperatures often top 100 degrees Fahrenheit during its long, hot summers. Arkansas winters tend to be short and mild. Little Rock's temperature reaches 50 degrees Fahrenheit on most winter days.

The state averages 50 inches of rain a year. Arkansas's mountains receive about 6 inches of snow a year.

*Overleaf: The state capitol, in Little Rock*

*From Ancient Times Until Today*

# From Ancient Times Until Today

Millions of years ago, nearly all of Arkansas was under water. Fish fossils have been found on Arkansas's now-dry land.

Many animals that no longer exist once lived in Arkansas. Mosasaurs were there. They were giant lizards. Huge wolves also lived in Arkansas. Mastodon bones were uncovered 20 feet below the ground in northeast Arkansas. Mastodons looked something like today's elephants.

## American Indians

People reached Arkansas at least 12,000 years ago. They were ancestors of today's American Indians. Some of these early Arkansans lived in caves along the White River. They made homes under rock shelves. These people are known as the Bluff Dwellers.

About 2,000 years ago, American Indians began building huge dirt mounds. In Arkansas, the mounds appeared near rivers. Some were burial places. Others were used as places of safety during

*French explorers Louis Jolliet and Father Jacques Marquette reached the mouth of the Arkansas River in 1673.*

floods. The Toltec Mounds are the tallest mounds in Arkansas. They are near Little Rock. They were built more than 1,000 years ago. The tallest mound is 50 feet high.

By the late 1600s, three large Indian groups lived in Arkansas. The Osages hunted in the north. The Caddos lived along the Red River in the south. The Quapaws built villages at the mouth of the Arkansas River. Many of these Indians built grass-roofed wooden houses. They grew corn and pumpkins and hunted deer and bears.

## EUROPEAN EXPLORERS AND SETTLERS

Hernando De Soto was the first known European in Arkansas. He arrived in 1541 and explored Arkansas for Spain. But the Spanish did not settle there.

French explorers reached Arkansas in the late 1600s. Louis Jolliet and Father Jacques Marquette

*The French helped coin the name Arkansas. They heard other Indians call the Quapaws the Akansea. The French changed this to Arkansea or Arkansas.*

15

*La Salle's full name was René-Robert Cavelier, Sieur de La Salle.*

*The area settled by De Tonti is now Arkansas Post National Memorial.*

canoed down the Mississippi River. In 1673, they arrived at the mouth of the Arkansas River. La Salle reached Arkansas in 1682. He visited a Quapaw Indian village. "We were well treated and given a cabin for our stay," wrote Henri de Tonti. He was La Salle's lieutenant.

La Salle claimed the Mississippi River valley for France. He named it Louisiana in honor of King Louis XIV of France. Arkansas was part of this land.

In 1686, Henri de Tonti returned to Arkansas. He founded Arkansas Post. It was a fur-trading post in southeast Arkansas. Arkansas Post became Arkansas's first permanent non-Indian settlement. De Tonti is called the "Father of Arkansas."

In 1717, several hundred German and Dutch settlers came to Arkansas Post. By 1721, most of them had left the area. During the next forty years, few Europeans settled in Arkansas.

By 1733, England had thirteen colonies along the Atlantic Ocean. From time to time, England and France fought to control North America. In 1762, the two countries were at war. The French were afraid they would lose Louisiana to the English. To keep this from happening, France turned the Louisiana lands over to Spain. This included Arkansas. Spain did nothing to settle the land. In 1800, France regained the land. By then, only about 400 non-Indian people lived in Arkansas.

## THE UNITED STATES STEPS IN

By 1783, England's thirteen colonies had become the United States. In the early 1800s, the new country wanted Louisiana. In 1803, the United States paid France $15 million for that land. Arkansas was part of this Louisiana Purchase.

Soon thousands of Americans were heading to Arkansas. They traveled in wagons. They also came down the Mississippi on flatboats. When they reached Arkansas, the pioneers built log cabins.

*After the Louisiana Purchase, thousands of American settlers headed to Arkansas.*

*Fort Smith National Historic Site*

They planted vegetables and fruit trees. Some settlers from southern states brought slaves. The slaves planted cotton and tobacco. These crops became important in the early 1800s.

New towns were begun. In 1807, Hot Springs was founded. The town grew around hot spring waters that bubbled from the ground. In 1812, William Lewis built a hut near a bluff. The French had called the bluff *petit roche*. That means "little rock." By 1820, the town of Little Rock was laid out there. Fort Smith began as a United States army post in 1817. The fort was built to keep the peace between Indian tribes.

In 1819, the United States Congress created the Arkansas Territory. All of what is now Arkansas was part of it. So was a piece of Oklahoma. Little Rock became the territory's capital in 1821. By 1836, Arkansas had 60,000 people. That was enough for statehood. Arkansas became the twenty-fifth state on June 15, 1836. Little Rock was the new state's capital.

Arkansas's Indians had to give up their land to the settlers. By 1840, the Indians had been moved to present-day Oklahoma.

The 1850s were good years for Arkansas. Much iron, lead, and coal were mined. Cotton plantations

were built along the Mississippi River. More slaves were brought to Arkansas to tend the cotton crops.

*The Old State House, Little Rock*

## THE CIVIL WAR

Like other southern states, Arkansas allowed slavery. By 1860, one-fourth of Arkansas's 435,450 people were black slaves. In that year, Abraham Lincoln was elected president. Southerners feared that he would end slavery. The southern states began to withdraw from the United States. They formed the Confederate States of America (the Confederacy).

*Only 4 of every 100 white Arkansans owned slaves. But those few people often owned many slaves.*

The Civil War (1861-1865) broke out in April 1861. It pitted the Confederacy (the South) against the Union (the North). President Lincoln asked for

*Union forces won the Battle of Pea Ridge in March 1862.*

*About 9,000 white Arkansans and 5,000 black Arkansans fought for the North.*

troops from Arkansas. Arkansans refused to fight fellow southerners. On May 6, 1861, Arkansas voted to leave the Union.

About 60,000 Arkansans served in the Confederate army. Two major Civil War battles were fought in northwest Arkansas. The Battle of Pea Ridge (March 6-8, 1862) was a Union victory. More than 25,000 soldiers took part in that battle. On December 7, 1862, the Confederates won the Battle of Prairie Grove.

Union forces captured Little Rock in September 1863. Two years later, the Union won the war. About 10,000 Arkansans had died in the fighting. The Union victory freed the slaves.

## RECONSTRUCTION, PROBLEMS, AND GROWTH

The southern states were not allowed to rejoin the United States right away. First, they had to go through Reconstruction. Each southern state had to show that it would grant black people their rights. Arkansas approved a new constitution in 1868. It granted black Arkansans the vote. Arkansas rejoined the United States on June 22, 1868. Only Tennessee reentered earlier.

Arkansans had trouble recovering from the Civil War. Thousands of freed slaves and poor whites became sharecroppers. They farmed other people's land. They had to share their crops with the landowners. Sharecroppers had little money. They could barely feed and clothe their families.

In the 1890s, white southerners began denying black people their rights. Black children were not allowed to attend the same schools as white children. Black adults were kept from voting. Sometimes black people were lynched (hanged without a trial). Altogether, more than 200 black Arkansans were lynched.

Yet Arkansas also moved forward in the late 1800s. The University of Arkansas opened at Fayetteville in 1872. The 1800s were big railroad-

*Bauxite is used to make aluminum.*

*John Huddleston (below) discovered diamonds on his land in 1906.*

building years in Arkansas. Trains took lumber, coal, and other Arkansas products to market. In 1887, bauxite was discovered near Little Rock. New people came to work in the state's growing industries. From 1870 to 1900, the number of Arkansans nearly tripled. By 1900, the population was 1,311,564.

Arkansas had continued growth in the early 1900s. In 1904, William Fuller grew Arkansas's first big rice crop. Soon rice was a major crop for the state. In 1906, John Huddleston saw two crystals in

his southwest Arkansas fields. They were diamonds. Huddleston's land became the country's only diamond mine.

## WORLD WARS AND DEPRESSION

The United States entered World War I (1914-1918) in 1917. That summer, Camp Pike was built near Little Rock. Within a short time, 100,000 soldiers were stationed at the base. That was more people than lived in Little Rock at the time. About 72,000 Arkansans helped win the war.

*Two thousand Arkansans were killed or wounded in World War I.*

In 1921, oil was discovered near El Dorado. Within months, nearly 500 wells were pumping oil. By 1924, Arkansas was the country's fourth-leading oil state.

Yet Arkansas was also one of the poorest states. Its people earned much less than most other Americans. Then, the Great Depression (1929-1939) hit the United States. This was a period of great hardship. It made life even worse for Arkansans. Thousands of them lost their farms. Many Arkansas factories closed.

World War II (1939-1945) helped end the Great Depression. Arkansas oil fueled machines used in the war. About 205,000 Arkansas men and

*General Douglas MacArthur, from Little Rock, was a World War II hero.*

women served in uniform. General Douglas MacArthur was a great war hero. The Little Rock native commanded the army in the Pacific. He oversaw the surrender of Japan on September 2, 1945. That ended the war.

## RECENT CHANGES

In 1954, the Supreme Court ruled that United States schools must be integrated. This meant that white students and black students would attend the same schools. By 1957, Little Rock's Central High School still didn't allow blacks. That September, nine black students tried to attend the school. White mobs blocked them. So did troops sent by Arkansas governor Orval Faubus. This went on for three weeks.

Finally, President Dwight Eisenhower sent soldiers to Little Rock. They walked the students into Central High on September 25, 1957. Southerners saw that the United States government was serious. It would use force to integrate the schools. By the 1970s, most Arkansas schools were integrated.

Arkansas was changing in other ways. In 1950, about 215,000 Arkansans farmed the land. That was almost four times the number farming today.

*In 1957, President Dwight D. Eisenhower sent federal troops to Little Rock to enforce integration of Central High School.*

Machines replaced thousands of the farm workers. Many of them tried to find factory jobs. But there were not enough jobs to go around. That caused large numbers of Arkansans to leave the state. Between 1940 and 1960, Arkansas lost nearly 200,000 people.

By 1960, industry passed farming at earning money in Arkansas. In recent years, Arkansas's rate of manufacturing growth has led the country. The state has become a major food producer. Its paper and cloth-making industries have also boomed.

*Senators John McClellan of Arkansas and Robert Kerr of Oklahoma sponsored the river project.*

Since 1971, the McClellan-Kerr Arkansas River Navigation System has helped this boom. The Arkansas River's channels were widened and deepened. Locks and dams were built on the river. Now, oceangoing vessels can ship goods in and out of Arkansas. Rapid growth has had its price. Arkansas's environment has suffered. Timber companies have completely cut down some Arkansas forests. Soil from stripped forests has muddied Arkansas's rivers. Many fish have been killed. The food industry has caused pollution, too. Wastes from chicken-processing plants and other factories have choked streams that used to be pure.

Poverty is another problem. Only three states are poorer than Arkansas. One-third of Arkansas's

children live in poverty. The state's level of health care is low. Arkansas's death rate is one of the country's highest.

Arkansas's leaders continue to work on the state's problems. They have brought new companies and more jobs to Arkansas. In the 1980s, they started programs to make their schools better. The school day and school year are now longer. Class sizes are smaller. High-school dropouts lose their driver's licenses. Today, Arkansas has the lowest school dropout rate in the South. Now, Arkansans look forward to the year 2000. They plan on the state being a Land of Opportunity for all.

*Even though industry has passed farming at earning money in Arkansas, about 6 billion pounds of rice are harvested each year.*

*Overleaf: A furniture maker at the Ozark Folk Center near Mountain View*

# Arkansans and Their Work

Arkansas has about 2.4 million people. The state ranks thirty-third among the fifty states in population. Four of every five Arkansans are white. One in six is black. About 20,000 Hispanic Americans, 13,000 American Indians, and 13,000 Asian Americans live in Arkansas. About half of all Arkansans live on farms or in small towns.

## Arkansans at Work

Almost one million Arkansans have jobs. That is nearly half the population. Manufacturing is the state's leading kind of job. About one-fourth of Arkansas's workers make goods. Foods are the top product. Riceland Foods is based in Stuttgart. The company makes Riceland rice. Tyson Foods is based in Springdale. It is the world's largest chicken packager. Other Arkansas products include paper, lumber, oil, refrigerators, cloth, and clothing.

Arkansas is a major farming state. About 65,000 people work on the state's 45,000 farms. Chickens are the state's number-one farm product. Arkansas

*About 375,000 black people live in Arkansas, and nearly 13,000 Asians.*

*Each year, Arkansas raises four times as many chickens as there are people in the United States. The state produces about one egg for each person on earth each year.*

*Arkansas ranks high in egg production (left) and sixth at growing cotton (right).*

raises a billion chickens each year. That is more than any other state. Most are eaten as meat. Some are raised to produce eggs. Arkansas also ranks high in egg production. Its chickens produce about 4 billion eggs each year. Arkansas ranks third among the states at raising turkeys.

About 6 billion pounds of rice are harvested in Arkansas each year. No other state grows more than half that much rice. Arkansas is one of the top ten soybean, grape, and pecan growers. The state ranks sixth at growing cotton.

Arkansas has more than 154,000 government workers. They include workers in Arkansas's three national forests and forty-eight state parks. Teachers and military people are other government workers. Fort Chaffee is a big army base. It is near the town of Fort Smith.

About 5,000 Arkansans work at mining. Natural gas is the top mining product. Oil is Arkansas's second-leading mining product. Arkansas leads the country at mining bromine. This element goes into dyes and medicines. Coal, clays, and sand and gravel are other Arkansas mining products.

*Teachers are among the 154,000 government workers in Arkansas.*

*Overleaf: Hot air balloons over the Little Rock skyline*

# A Tour of Arkansas

# A Tour of Arkansas

Arkansas is a beautiful state to visit. People go there to enjoy the hot springs and the Ozark Mountains. They also visit its cities and small towns.

## The Little Rock Area

*The Arkansas Gazette print shop at the Arkansas Territorial Restoration in Little Rock*

Little Rock is a good place to start an Arkansas tour. This city is near the state's center. Little Rock has been Arkansas's capital since 1821. It is the state's largest city, with more than 175,000 people.

The Arkansas Territorial Restoration is in Little Rock. The buildings there show life in Arkansas before the Civil War. The Hinderliter House is Little Rock's oldest structure. It was made of logs in the 1820s. William Woodruff's home and print shop is also there. Woodruff founded the *Arkansas Gazette* at Arkansas Post in 1819. Two years later, he moved the newspaper to Little Rock. The *Gazette* was printed until 1991. It was the oldest newspaper west of the Mississippi River.

The Old State House in Little Rock is made of handmade brick. Arkansas's government met there

for seventy-five years (1836-1911). Today, it is a museum of Arkansas history.

The present state capitol has been in use since 1911. It was modeled after the United States Capitol in Washington, D.C. However, it is only one-fourth as big. The Arkansas Vietnam Veterans Memorial is on the capitol grounds. It honors the 600 Arkansans who died in the Vietnam War.

Little Rock's parks contain many landmarks. Riverfront Park lies along the Arkansas River. The "little rock" for which Little Rock was named is there.

MacArthur Park was named for General Douglas MacArthur. His birthplace is in the park.

*Above: The Brownlee-Noland House, Arkansas Territorial Restoration
Below: The Museum of Science and History, in MacArthur Park*

*Tigers at the Little Rock Zoo*

*Little Rock Air Force Base*

Today, the birthplace is the Arkansas Museum of Science and History. Confederate general Albert Pike's home is near MacArthur Park. The Decorative Arts Museum is now in Pike's home. Quilts, baskets, and other crafts are displayed there.

The Little Rock Zoo is in War Memorial Park. The zoo is noted for its apes. They live in a natural setting. The home field of the Arkansas Travelers is also in the park. They are a minor-league baseball team.

Little Rock has a "twin city" across the Arkansas River. This is North Little Rock. About 62,000 people live there. That makes North Little Rock the state's third-largest city. North Little Rock has its own Riverfront Park. A big sundial is in the park. It was built in 1986 to honor the state's 150th birthday.

A few miles northeast is Jacksonville. Little Rock Air Force Base is there. Pilots learn to fly cargo planes at the base. These aircraft deliver food and supplies to needy people around the world.

SOUTHERN ARKANSAS

Hot Springs is southwest of Little Rock. The city was named for the hot water that bubbles out of the ground. Rainwater drips through the ground. About 1 mile underground, the water hits very hot rocks. Then, it works its way back aboveground. The water is 143 degrees Fahrenheit when it comes out of the ground. Water from the springs is piped to bathhouses. It is cooled to about 100 degrees Fahrenheit so people can bathe in it. Millions of bathers have enjoyed the soothing waters of Hot Springs.

In 1921, the land with the bubbling waters became Hot Springs National Park. It is the only national park almost completely inside a city. The

*Bath House Row, Hot Springs National Park*

park has forty-seven springs. Each day, about 1 million gallons of water flow from them.

The Mid-America Museum is also in Hot Springs. This science museum has an outdoor aquarium. It is filled with freshwater fish that are native to Arkansas. The museum also has hands-on exhibits about weather and flying.

Magnet Cove is just east of Hot Springs. Scientists have counted more than 100 kinds of minerals there. One of them is magnetite. It acts like a magnet and attracts metal objects.

Murfreesboro is southwest of Hot Springs. In the early 1900s, North America's only diamond mine was there. Today, Crater of Diamonds State Park is found there. For a small price, visitors may look for diamonds. They may keep any they find. About 1,000 diamonds are found each year. The largest one was the "Uncle Sam." It is worth $250,000.

Hope is south of the diamond mine. President Bill Clinton was born in Hope. Two of his childhood homes can be seen there. Hope is also Arkansas's "Watermelon Capital." The Watermelon Festival is held there each August. A prize is given for the largest watermelon. The winner generally weighs about 200 pounds.

*Visitors to Crater of Diamonds State Park may keep any diamonds they find.*

Twin cities named Texarkana lie at the Arkansas-Texas border. Texarkana, Arkansas, has about 23,000 people. Texarkana, Texas, has about 32,000 people. The name *Texarkana* has parts of three states' names. They are *Tex*as, *Ark*ansas, and Louisi*ana*. State Line Avenue divides the two cities. The street runs through the post office that is shared by the cities.

East of Texarkana is El Dorado. Much oil comes from the El Dorado area. So does bromine. It is found in salty water called brine. The Arkansas Oil and Brine Museum shows how oil and bromine are mined. The museum is to the north in Smackover.

Felsenthal National Wildlife Refuge is east of El Dorado. The refuge is known for its waterbirds. Great blue herons and snowy egrets can be seen there. River otters and beavers also live at the refuge.

Pine Bluff is north of the refuge. In 1819, Joseph Bonne built a home there. It was high above the Arkansas River. Pine trees grew there. Today, Pine Bluff has more than 57,000 people. It is the fourth-largest city in Arkansas. Paper and wood products are made in Pine Bluff. Cotton grown nearby is shipped there. Boats on the Arkansas River move goods in and out of Pine Bluff. Trains carry

*State Line Avenue divides the cities of Texarkana, Arkansas, and Texarkana, Texas.*

*Workers on the Arkansas River at Pine Bluff load flour for export.*

*Stuttgart is in Arkansas County. Only two counties in the country grow more rice than Arkansas County. Both are in California.*

*Musicians at the Ozark Mountain Folk Festival in Mountain View*

many goods there also. The Arkansas Railroad Museum is at Pine Bluff. It shows how railroads helped Arkansas grow.

To the northeast is Stuttgart. This town was founded by Germans in 1878. Today, it is known as Arkansas's "Rice Capital." The Stuttgart Agricultural Museum tells the story of rice farming.

## NORTHERN ARKANSAS

Blytheville is in northeast Arkansas. During the 1500s, Indians built large mounds there. Today, Blytheville is an important farming and trading

town. It is also home to Mississippi County Community College. All power for the school comes from solar cells.

Jonesboro is west of Blytheville. It is Arkansas's fifth-largest city. Almost 47,000 people live there. About 300 are Muslims. Their house of prayer is called a mosque. Arkansas's only mosque is in Jonesboro. It is close to Arkansas State University. The university's museum has a fine prehistoric Indian exhibit.

*A woodcarver at the Ozark Folk Center, near Mountain View*

Mountain View is west of Jonesboro in the Ozark Mountains. Ozark Folk Center State Park is at Mountain View. Arts and crafts from the 1800s are demonstrated there. Workers make candles, baskets, and quilts. They also fashion apple-head dolls and cornhusk dolls. Each September, the Arkansas State Fiddler's Contest is held there.

Blanchard Springs Caverns is a few miles north of Mountain View. Elevators take visitors down to these caves. Trails lead through an underground world of rock formations. One of the caves is the Cathedral Room. It is the size of four football fields laid end to end.

To the northeast is Mammoth Spring State Park. It is just south of the Missouri border. Mammoth Spring produces 234 million gallons of

*A twilight view of Eureka Springs*

*The University of Arkansas also has branches at Little Rock, Pine Bluff, and Monticello.*

water each day. That is enough to fill more than 300 Olympic-size swimming pools.

Eureka Springs is in northwest Arkansas. More than sixty cold-water springs bubble from the ground. Many visitors enjoy walking down the town's steep streets. They see stone and brick buildings that date from the 1880s. Some visitors fish in nearby Beaver Lake.

Pea Ridge National Military Park is north of Eureka Springs. A great Civil War battle took place there. Elkhorn Tavern, where the fighting ended, has been restored. Nearby is the town of Pea Ridge. Its streets are named for the men who fought in the battle.

Fayetteville is southwest of the battlefield. It is the main home of the University of Arkansas. That is the state's largest school. About 14,000 students attend there. The university has a history and science museum. The museum displays a 5-pound meteorite. This large rock from space fell near Fayetteville in 1934.

South of Fayetteville is Fort Smith. That is a good place to end an Arkansas tour. This city began as an army fort in 1817. Today, nearly 75,000 people live there. It is Arkansas's second-largest city. Fort Smith is called the "Industrial Capital of

Arkansas." Many items are made there. They include furniture and packaged peanuts.

Many visitors go to the Fort Smith National Historic Site. They can see Judge Isaac Parker's courtroom and jail. From 1875 to 1896, Parker was called the "hanging judge." He ordered nearly 100 gunfighters and outlaws to be hanged.

The Fort Smith Art Center is in an 1879 house. It has paintings and other works by artists from around Arkansas. Barry Thomas's work has been shown at the center. Thomas played football for the University of Arkansas Razorbacks. Later, he became a well-known artist for Walt Disney movies.

*Elkhorn Tavern, at Pea Ridge National Military Park, has been restored.*

A Gallery of Famous Arkansans

# A GALLERY OF FAMOUS ARKANSANS

Arkansas has produced many famous people. They include baseball stars, authors, and a president.

Sarasen (1735?-1832) was Arkansas's last Quapaw Indian chief. He is remembered for his kindness toward white settlers. Chickasaw Indians stole two children from a trapper's family. Sarasen followed their trail. He found the children and rescued them. On his tombstone in Pine Bluff is written: "Rescuer of Captive Children." After Sarasen's death, Arkansas's remaining Quapaws were sent to Oklahoma.

Roberta Waugh Fulbright (1874-1953) was born in Missouri. Later, she and her husband moved to Arkansas. He died in 1923. Fulbright had six children to raise. She also ran a newspaper, the *Fayetteville Democrat.* Fulbright wrote a column for the paper. It was called "As I See It." The paper is now the *Northwest Arkansas Times.*

Hattie Caraway (1878-1950) was born in Tennessee. She was married to Arkansas senator Thaddeus Caraway. He died in 1931. Caraway was appointed to serve the rest of his term. In

*Opposite: Arkansas native President Bill Clinton (left) with Vice President Al Gore*

*Hattie Caraway*

November 1932, she was elected to the U.S. Senate. Caraway was the first woman elected as a U.S. senator. She served two terms (1933-1945). She was also the first woman to chair a Senate committee.

**James William Fulbright** was born in Missouri in 1905. His mother was Roberta Waugh Fulbright. Young Fulbright grew up in Fayetteville. He entered the University of Arkansas when he was only sixteen. Later, he became the university's president (1939-1941). Fulbright then served Arkansas in the U.S. Congress. First, he was a representative (1943-1945). Fulbright then replaced Hattie Caraway in the Senate (1945-1974). In 1946, he

*Fulbright Scholarships are named for Arkansas native Senator James William Fulbright.*

helped pass the Fulbright Act. This law created Fulbright Scholarships. They help people study in other lands. By 1993, about 160,000 "Fulbrights" had been granted.

**William Jefferson "Bill" Clinton** was born at Hope in 1946. He grew up there and in Hot Springs. Clinton wanted to become a great lawmaker like James William Fulbright. He graduated from Yale University Law School in 1973. Clinton then taught law at the University of Arkansas (1973-1976). In 1979, Clinton became Arkansas's youngest governor. He served for twelve years (1979-1981 and 1983-1993). In 1993, Clinton became the third-youngest president in United States history. The forty-second president plans to create more jobs. He also wants to improve the country's schools and health care.

*Only Presidents Theodore Roosevelt and John F. Kennedy were younger than Clinton.*

**M. Joycelyn Elders** was born in Schaal in 1933. Her poor sharecropper family had little medical care. Elders decided she would one day be a doctor. Her parents and seven younger brothers and sisters picked cotton to send her to college. She became a pediatrician. Dr. Elders headed the Arkansas Department of Health from 1987 to 1993. In 1993, President Clinton appointed her surgeon general of the United States.

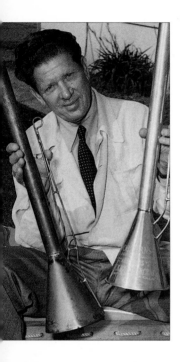

*Bob Burns, with the bazookas he invented*

*A weapon that fires rockets is also called a bazooka. Because of its shape, this weapon was named after Bob Burns' musical instrument.*

**Scott Joplin** (1868-1917) was born in Texarkana, Texas. He went to Orr School in Texarkana, Arkansas. Later, Joplin helped start ragtime music. One of his well-known songs is "Maple Leaf Rag."

**Sanford Faulkner** (1803-1874) lived in Chicot County. He had a cotton plantation there. Around 1840, Faulkner made up a song called "The Arkansaw Traveler." The song's story tells of a traveler seeking a place to stay. The traveler stops at a farmer's cabin. The farmer just pokes fun at him. Finally, the traveler picks up a fiddle and plays a tune. The farmer and traveler become friends through music. "The Arkansaw Traveler" became a popular song and story.

**Bob Burns** (1890-1956) was born in Greenwood. When he was fifteen, Burns invented the "bazooka." He slid one metal tube into another and blew into it. This was a new musical instrument. Later, Burns hosted a radio show. It was called "The Arkansas Traveler." On it, he played his bazooka. He also told stories about Grandpa Snazzy and Uncle Pud. They were his imaginary Arkansas relatives.

**Florence Price** (1888-1953) was born in Little Rock. She published a piece of music when she was eleven. Price became the first famous black woman composer. Her best-known piece is "My Soul's Been Anchored in the Lord." This is a spiritual. Price also wrote symphonies.

**William Warfield** was born in West Helena in 1920. He became an opera singer and actor. In the movie *Show Boat,* he sang "Old Man River." He also played the role of Porgy in *Porgy and Bess.*

**Dee Brown** was born in Louisiana in 1908. He grew up in Stephens and Little Rock. Brown sometimes went to Western movies with Indian friends. "Those aren't real Indians," they told him. Later, he wrote books about the Old West. *Bury My Heart at Wounded Knee* is told from the Indian point of view. It has sold five million copies in seventeen languages.

**Sam Walton** (1918-1992) was born in Oklahoma. He later moved to Arkansas. In 1962, he began a chain of stores. His first Wal-Mart was in

*Sam Walton, accepting an honor from President George Bush*

*Daisy Gatson Bates*

*Maya Angelou*

Rogers, Arkansas. The chain's headquarters is in Bentonville. By 1992, Wal-Mart was the world's largest retail chain. Walton was one of the richest Americans. Today, 380,000 people work in 2,000 Walton stores.

**John H. Johnson** was born in Arkansas City in 1918. He moved to Chicago, Illinois, as a teenager. In 1942, Johnson began the *Negro Digest*. Many people thought a magazine for black people would not sell. He later founded *Jet* and *Ebony* magazines.

**Daisy Gatson Bates** was born in Huttig in 1922. She became a civil-rights leader. She was married to **L. C. Bates** (1901-1981). In 1941, they founded the *Arkansas State Press* in Little Rock. Their newspaper fought for black people's rights. Daisy Gatson Bates helped integrate Arkansas's schools. In 1957, she led nine black students into Little Rock's Central High. In 1987, a Little Rock school was named for her.

**Maya Angelou** was born in Missouri in 1928. She grew up in Stamps, Arkansas. Angelou became a dancer, actress, teacher, and author. Her best-known book is *I Know Why the Caged Bird Sings*. It tells of her childhood in Arkansas. In 1992, Angelou was asked to write a special poem. She read it at President Clinton's 1993 inauguration.

Johnny Cash was born near Kingsland in 1932. His family moved to Dyess. They farmed cotton there. By the time he was twelve, Cash was writing songs. He became a famous country singer and songwriter. One of his best-known songs is "I Walk the Line." He helped make country music popular throughout the United States. **Glen Campbell** is another famous country singer. He was born in Delight, Arkansas, in 1938. "Gentle on My Mind" is one of his well-known songs.

Arkansas has also produced many sports stars. **Jay Hannah "Dizzy" Dean** (1911-1974) was born in Lucas. He and brother **Paul "Daffy" Dean**

*Glen Campbell*

*Dizzy (left) and Daffy Dean (right) pose with Detroit Tiger pitcher Schoolboy Rowe at the 1934 World Series.*

*Lou Brock*

(1913-1981) both became major-league pitchers. For many years, they both pitched for the St. Louis Cardinals. In 1934, Dizzy won thirty-two games and Daffy won twenty-one. That included the two World Series games they each won. In 1953, Dizzy was elected to the Baseball Hall of Fame.

**Brooks Robinson** was born in Little Rock in 1937. He played third base for the Baltimore Orioles. Robinson won sixteen Gold Glove awards (1960-1975) for his fielding. He also hit 268 home runs in his career. In 1982, he was elected to the Baseball Hall of Fame.

**Lou Brock** was born in El Dorado in 1939. He also played for the St. Louis Cardinals. Brock turned base stealing into an art. He stole at least fifty bases twelve years straight. That is a major-league record. Brock is another Arkansan in the Baseball Hall of Fame.

**Scottie Pippen** was born in Hamburg, Arkansas, in 1965. He loved to play basketball. But he nearly quit his Hamburg High School team. Pippen was a benchwarmer at first. He went on to star at Central Arkansas University. Then he joined the Chicago Bulls. His great scoring and defense helped the Bulls become winners. In 1991, 1992, and 1993, the Bulls were world champions.

*Basketball star Scottie Pippen is a member of the three-time NBA champion Chicago Bulls.*

The birthplace of Scottie Pippen, Daisy Bates, Florence Price, Dizzy Dean, and Bill Clinton . . .

Home also to Chief Sarasen, Sam Walton, Hattie Caraway, and Maya Angelou . . .

The top state for raising chickens and growing rice . . .

A land of hot springs, diamonds, and the Ozark Mountains . . .

This is Arkansas—the Land of Opportunity.

# Did You Know?

If all the eggs produced in Arkansas each year were placed end to end, they would reach almost halfway to the moon.

**In the 1800s, some people wrote the state's name *Arkansaw*. Others spelled it *Arkansas*. Some said *Ar-KAN-zus*. Others pronounced it *AR-kun-saw*. In 1881, the state legislature ruled that it should be pronounced AR-kun-saw but written Arkansas.**

Razorback hogs were said to be wild hogs with sharp ridges on their backs. Some Arkansas men claimed to have shaved with the bony ridge. Actually, razorback hogs never existed. Still, the University of Arkansas sports teams are called the Razorbacks.

Evening Shade, Magazine, Okay, Toad Suck, Tomato, Strawberry, and Umpire are all Arkansas towns.

**"Fried pies" are a favorite Arkansas food. Dried apples and peaches are folded into a pastry crust. They are then golden fried. President Bill Clinton loves them.**

**Yellville was named for Archibald Yell, an Arkansas governor. Each October, Yellville hosts the National Wild Turkey Calling Contest.**

If cooked in one place, Arkansas's yearly rice harvest could fill a building five times the size of the Sears Tower (the world's tallest building).

In 1987, Arkansas named the vine-ripened pink tomato grown in southern Arkansas the state fruit and vegetable. The tomato is really a fruit. However, most people think of it as a vegetable.

I. Q. Zoo is at Hot Springs. Highly trained animals can be seen in action. A parrot roller skates. A raccoon shoots the correct number of baskets to answer math questions. Visitors can also watch a chicken dance while a rabbit plays the piano and a duck strums a guitar.

Have you ever wondered why the names *Arkansas* and *Kansas* are similar? The states were named for tribes with similar names. Kansas was named for the Kansa Indians; Arkansas for the Akansea, or Quapaw, Indians.

**The World Championship Mosquito Calling Contest is held in Walcott, Arkansas, each August. People dress as mosquitoes. There is also a prize for the tastiest recipe using mosquitoes. But it's not easy finding judges.**

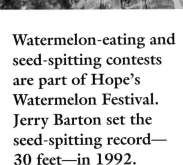

**Watermelon-eating and seed-spitting contests are part of Hope's Watermelon Festival. Jerry Barton set the seed-spitting record— 30 feet—in 1992.**

Arkansas cotton farmers used to say they worked "from can to can't." They meant from sunrise, when farmers can see to work, to nighttime, when they can't see their fields any longer.

**Baseball Hall of Fame shortstop Joseph Floyd Vaughan hit .318 for his career. He was called Arky Vaughan because his birthplace was Clifty, Arkansas.**

# Arkansas Information

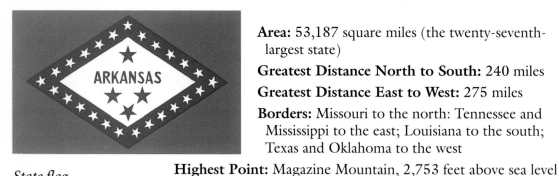

**Area:** 53,187 square miles (the twenty-seventh-largest state)

**Greatest Distance North to South:** 240 miles

**Greatest Distance East to West:** 275 miles

**Borders:** Missouri to the north: Tennessee and Mississippi to the east; Louisiana to the south; Texas and Oklahoma to the west

*State flag*

*Mockingbird*

*Fiddle*

**Highest Point:** Magazine Mountain, 2,753 feet above sea level

**Lowest Point:** Along the southern border at the Ouachita River, 55 feet above sea level

**Hottest Recorded Temperature:** 120° F. (at Ozark, on August 10, 1936)

**Coldest Recorded Temperature:** -29° F. (Pond in Benton County, on February 13, 1905)

**Statehood:** The twenty-fifth state, on June 15, 1836

**Origin of Name:** *Akansea*, meaning "south wind," was another name for the Quapaw Indians; the French called them *Arkansea* or *Arkansas*

**Capital:** Little Rock (since 1821)

**Counties:** 75

**United States Senators:** 2

**United States Representatives:** 4 (as of 1992)

**State Senators:** 35

**State Representatives:** 100

**State Song:** "Arkansas," by Eva Ware Barnett

**State Motto:** *Regnat Populus* (Latin, meaning "the people rule")

**Nicknames:** "Land of Opportunity," "Wonder State," "Bear State," "Natural State"

**State Seal:** Adopted in 1907

**State Flag:** Adopted in 1913

**State Flower:** Apple blossom

**State Bird:** Mockingbird

**State Tree:** Pine

**State Insect:** Honeybee

**State Instrument:** Fiddle

**State Gem:** Diamond

**State Drink:** Milk

**State Fruit and Vegetable:** Vine-ripened pink tomato

**Some Rivers:** Mississippi, Arkansas, Ouachita, Red, Black, White, St. Francis

**Some Lakes:** Ouachita, Millwood, Greers Ferry, Beaver, Bull Shoals, Norfolk, Table Rock, Chicot

**Wildlife:** Black bears, deer, bobcats, armadillos, alligators, red foxes, opossums, raccoons, woodchucks, squirrels, rabbits, mockingbirds, whippoorwills, blue jays, cardinals, robins, woodpeckers, ducks, wild turkeys, trout, catfish, other kinds of fish, water moccasins, other kinds of snakes

**Manufactured Products:** Packaged chicken, rice, soft drinks, cardboard, paper bags, lumber, refined oil, refrigerators, television sets, lightbulbs, air conditioners, cloth and clothing

**Farm Products:** Chickens, eggs, turkeys, beef cattle, dairy cattle, rice, soybeans, grapes, pecans, cotton, wheat, watermelons, pink tomatoes, sorghum

**Mining Products:** Natural gas, oil, bromine, coal, clays, sand and gravel, crushed stone

**Population:** 2,350,725, thirty-third among the states (1990 U.S. Census Bureau figures)

**Major Cities** (1990 Census):

| Little Rock | 175,795 | Fayetteville | 42,099 |
|---|---|---|---|
| Fort Smith | 72,798 | Hot Springs | 32,462 |
| North Little Rock | 61,741 | Springdale | 29,941 |
| Pine Bluff | 57,140 | Jacksonville | 29,101 |
| Jonesboro | 46,535 | West Memphis | 28,259 |

*Apple blossom*

*Cardinal*

*Raccoon*

# Arkansas History

*Henri de Tonti founded Arkansas Post in 1686.*

10,000 B.C.—Ancient Indians first reach Arkansas

1541—Hernando De Soto explores Arkansas for Spain

1673—Louis Jolliet and Father Jacques Marquette explore the Mississippi River valley as far south as the Arkansas River for France

1682—René-Robert Cavelier, Sieur de La Salle, claims the Mississippi River valley, including Arkansas, for France and names the area Louisiana

1686—Henri de Tonti helps found Arkansas Post, the region's first permanent non-Indian settlement

1762—France gives Spain control of Louisiana, including Arkansas

1800—France regains control of Louisiana, including Arkansas; Arkansas's non-Indian population is only about 400

1803—The United States purchases Louisiana, including Arkansas, from France

1807—The first permanent settlers reach Hot Springs

1812—The first settler arrives in Little Rock

1817—Fort Smith is begun

1819—The Arkansas Territory is created; the first Arkansas newspaper, the *Arkansas Gazette,* is founded

1836—Arkansas becomes the twenty-fifth state on June 15

1860—One-fourth of Arkansas's 435,450 population are black slaves

1861—The Civil War begins April 12; Arkansas leaves the Union May 6 and then joins the Confederacy

1862—The Battles of Pea Ridge and Prairie Grove are fought in Arkansas

1865—The Union wins the Civil War

1868—Arkansas is readmitted to the United States on June 22

1872—The University of Arkansas opens at Fayetteville

1874—The state constitution that is still in effect is adopted

1887—Bauxite, used in making aluminum, is found near Little Rock

1898—About 100 people die in a tornado at Fort Smith

1904—William Fuller grows Arkansas's first big rice crop

1906—Diamonds are found near Murfreesboro

1911—Arkansas's state capitol at Little Rock is completed

1913—Arkansas's state flag is adopted

1917-18—After the United States enters World War I, almost 72,000 Arkansans serve

1921—Oil is discovered near El Dorado

1927—Rainstorms flood one-fifth of Arkansas

1929-39—During the Great Depression, many Arkansas farms and factories go out of business

1932—Hattie Caraway of Arkansas is the first woman elected a U.S. senator

1941-45—After the United States enters World War II, about 205,000 Arkansas men and women serve

1946—Bill Clinton is born in Hope

1957—U.S. troops are sent to Little Rock to make sure that Central High School admits black students

1960s—Industry passes farming as the biggest moneymaker in Arkansas

1971—The McClellan-Kerr Arkansas River Navigation System opens

1978—Bill Clinton is elected governor

1986—Arkansas celebrates 150 years of statehood

1990—The Land of Opportunity's population is 2,350,725

1992—Bill Clinton is elected the forty-second president of the United States

*The worst flood in Arkansas history occurred in 1927.*

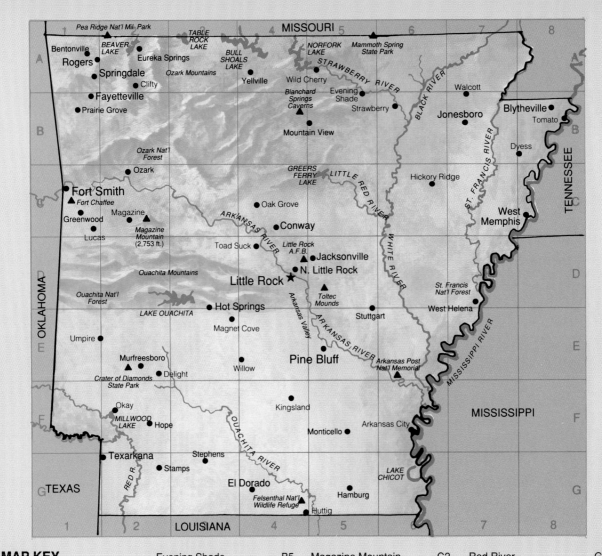

## MAP KEY

# GLOSSARY

**ancient:** Relating to a time early in history

**artificial:** Made by people; not occurring naturally

**bazooka:** A musical instrument invented by Bob Burns of Arkansas; a rocket-firing weapon named after Burns' invention

**billion:** A thousand million (1,000,000,000)

**capital:** The city that is the seat of government; a place known for a certain product, such as the "Rice Capital"

**capitol:** The building in which the government meets

**climate:** The typical weather of a region

**constitution:** The framework of government

**environment:** The climate, air, soil, and other living things that surround us

**explorer:** A person who visits and studies unknown lands

**fossil:** The hardened remains of animals or plants that lived long ago

**inauguration:** The act of officially taking office

**industry:** A business that uses many workers to make products

**integrate:** To bring people of various races together

**manufacturing:** The making of products

**mastodon:** A prehistoric animal in the elephant family

**million:** A thousand thousand (1,000,000)

**mosasaur:** A giant lizard that no longer exists

**mouth** (of a river): the place where one river empties into a larger body of water

**opportunity:** A good chance for success

**permanent:** Lasting

**plain:** Rather level land

**pollution:** The harming or dirtying of the environment

**population:** The number of people in a place

**prehistoric:** Belonging to the time before written history

**Reconstruction:** The period after the Civil War when the governments of the southern states and way of life in the South were reshaped

**segregate:** To keep people apart because of race or other reasons

**sharecropper:** A person who farms another person's land and shares the crops with that person

**slavery:** A practice in which some people are owned by other people

**spring** (of water): Water that bubbles out of the ground

**territory:** Land owned by a country; when used with a capital "T," such as Arkansas Territory, a region that is owned by a country and that has its own government

**wildlife refuge:** A place where animals are protected

PICTURE ACKNOWLEDGMENTS

Front cover, © Gene Ahrens; 1, © Tim Ernst; 2, Tom Dunnington; 3, © Buddy Mays/Travel Stock; 5, Tom Dunnington; 6-7, © Tim Ernst; 8, © Tim Ernst; 9 (left), © Tom Till; 9 (right), Courtesy Hammond, Incorporated, Maplewood, New Jersey; 10, © Tom Murphy/SuperStock; 11 (left), © Tim Ernst; 11 (right), Arkansas Dept. of Parks & Tourism, photo by A.C. Haralson; 12-13, John Elk/Tony Stone Images, Inc.; 15, North Wind Picture Archives, hand-colored; 17, North Wind Picture Archives, hand-colored; 18, Garry D. McMichael/Root Resources; 19, © Les Riess/Photri, Inc.; 20, Arkansas History Commission; 22, Arkansas History Commission; 24, Wide World Photos, Inc.; 25, AP/Wide World Photos; 27, © Garry D. McMichael/Root Resources; 28, © Bob Krist/Tony Stone Images, Inc.; 29 (top), © Mark Morgan; 29 (bottom), Arkansas Dept. of Parks & Tourism, photo by A.C. Haralson; 30 (both pictures), © Garry McMichael/Root Resources; 31, © Mark Morgan; 32-33, Arkansas Dept. of Parks & Tourism, photo by A.C. Haralson; 34, © Jean Higgins/N E Stock Photo; 35 (both pictures), © Jean Higgins/N E Stock Photo; 36 (both pictures), © Mark Morgan; 37, © Buddy Mays/Travel Stock; 38, © Buddy Mays/Travel Stock; 39 (top), Arkansas Dept. of Parks & Tourism, photo by A.C. Haralson; 39 (bottom), © Garry McMichael/Root Resources; 40, © Garry McMichael/Root Resources; 41, © Buddy Mays/Travel Stock; 42, © Bob Krist/Tony Stone Images, Inc.; 43, © Terry Donnelly/Tony Stone Images, Inc.; 44, AP/Wide World Photos; 45, AP/Wide World Photos; 46, Wide World Photos, Inc.; 48, AP/Wide world Photos; 49, Wide World Photos, Inc.; 50 (both pictures), AP/Wide World Photos; 51 (both pictures), AP/Wide World Photos; 52, AP/Wide World Photos; 53, Wide World Photos, Inc.; 54, © Camerique/H. Armstrong Roberts; 55 (top), Arkansas Department of Parks & Tourism, photo by A.C. Haralson; 55 (bottom), Courtesy of the Educated Animal Zoo; 56 (top), Courtesy Flag Research Center, Winchester, Massachusetts 01890; 56 (middle), © Ted Farrington/Root Resources; 56 (bottom), © J. Novak/Photri, Inc.; 57 (top), © Margo Taussig Pinkerton/N E Stock Photo; 57 (middle), © Richard Piliero/N E Stock Photo; 57 (bottom), © Robert Llewellyn/SuperStock; 58, Arkansas History Commission; 59, University of Arkansas at Little Rock Archives; 60, Tom Dunnington; back cover, © Terry Donnelly/Tom Stack and Associates

# INDEX

*Page numbers in boldface type indicate illustrations.*

## ABOUT THE AUTHORS

Dennis and Judith Fradin have coauthored several books in the From Sea to Shining Sea series. The Fradins both graduated from Northwestern University in 1967. Dennis has been a professional writer for twenty years, and has published 150 books. His works for Childrens Press include the Young People's Stories of Our States series, the Disaster! series, and the Thirteen Colonies series. Judith earned her M.A. in literature from Northwestern University and taught high school and college English for many years. The Fradins, who are the parents of Anthony, Diana, and Michael, live in Evanston, Illinois.